Happy Birthday Jo
from Jean
1973

Treasures of Inspiration

TREASURES

A Keepsake of Beautiful
Photographs and Writing

OF INSPIRATION

Edited by
Mary Dawson Hughes

♔ *Hallmark Crown Editions*

Acknowledgments

"Young Trees" by Frances Frost. Reprinted by permission of N. Carr Grace, Executrix for the Estate of Frances Frost. "Vision" by Kahlil Gibran from *A Second Treasury of Kahlil Gibran,* translated from the Arabic by Anthony R. Ferris. Copyright © 1962 by The Citadel Press. Reprinted by permission of The Citadel Press. "Good Morning, America" by Carl Sandburg from *Complete Poems.* Copyright 1950 by Harcourt Brace and World. Reprinted by permission of Harcourt Brace Jovanovich. "If" by Rudyard Kipling. Copyright © 1910 by Rudyard Kipling. Reprinted by permission of Doubleday and Company. Excerpt by Anne Frank from *Anne Frank: The Diary of a Young Girl.* Copyright 1952 by Otto Frank. Reprinted by permission of Doubleday and Company. "The Art of Living Each Day" by Wilferd A. Peterson from *More About the Art of Living.* Copyright © 1966 by Wilferd A. Peterson. Reprinted by permission of Simon & Schuster, Inc. "The Making of Friends" by Edgar A. Guest. Reprinted by permission of Henry Regnery Company. Excerpt from "The House by the Side of the Road" from *Dreams in Homespun* by Sam Walter Foss. Reprinted by permission of Lothrop, Lee & Shepard Company. "Will There Really be a 'Morning'"? by Emily Dickinson. Reprinted by permission of the publishers and the Trustees of Amherst College from Thomas H. Johnson, Editor, *The Poems of Emily Dickinson,* Cambridge, Mass.: The Belknap Press of Harvard University Press, Copyright, 1951, 1955, by The President and Fellows of Harvard College. "Clear Skies Again" from *Poems* by Boris Pasternak, 2d. enl. rev. ed., Antioch Press, 1964. Reprinted by permission of Eugene M. Kayden. "The Right Kind of People" by Edwin Markham. Reprinted by permission of Virgil Markham. Psalm 121 from the *King James Version Bible.* Reprinted by permission of Cambridge University Press. "The Lake Isle of Innisfree" from *Collected Poems* by William Butler Yeats. Copyright 1906 by The Macmillan Company, renewed 1934 by William Butler Yeats. Reprinted by permission of The Macmillan Company, M. B. Yeats, and the Macmillan Company of Canada. "Sea Fever" from *Poems* by John Masefield. Copyright 1912 by The Macmillan Company, renewed 1940 by John Masefield. Reprinted by permission of The Macmillan Company. Excerpt from "Night" by Sara Teasdale from *Collected Poems.* Copyright 1930 by Sara Teasdale Filsinger, renewed 1958 by Guaranty Trust Company of New York, Executor. Reprinted with permission of The Macmillan Company.

Treasures of Inspiration

The Art of Living Each Day / WILFERD A. PETERSON

$\mathcal{E}$ach day is a lifetime in miniature... To awaken each morning is to be born again, to fall asleep at night is to die to the day. In between waking and sleeping are the golden hours of the day. What we cannot do for a lifetime

we can do for a daytime. "Anyone," wrote Robert Louis Stevenson, "can live sweetly, patiently, lovingly, purely, till the sun goes down." Anyone can hold his temper for a day and guard the words he speaks. Anyone can carry his burden heroically for one day. Anyone can strive to be happy for a day and to spread happiness around. Anyone can radiate love for a day.

Anyone can rise above fear for a day and meet each situation with courage. Anyone can be kind and thoughtful and considerate for a day. Anyone can endeavor to learn something new each day and mark some growth. When we fail and fall short, let us forgive ourselves and consider the words of Emerson: "Finish every day and be done with it. Tomorrow is a new day; you will begin it well and serenely and with too high a spirit to be cumbered by your old nonsense." Live a day at a time and remember that tomorrow is another today.

The Child's Question

EMILY DICKINSON

Will there really be a "Morning"?
Is there such a thing as "Day"?
Could I see it from the mountains
If I were as tall as they?

Has it feet like Water lilies?
Has it feathers like a Bird?
Is it brought from famous countries
Of which I have never heard?

Oh, some Scholar! Oh, some Sailor,
Oh, some Wise Man from the skies!
Please to tell a little Pilgrim
Where the place called "Morning" lies?

If a man does not keep pace with his companions, perhaps it is because he hears a different drummer.

HENRY DAVID THOREAU

Young Trees

FRANCES FROST

A young tree standing
Slim and still
Is a tall green flower
On a quiet hill.

A young tree bending
Along a lane
Is a green flame blowing
In wind and rain.

A young tree growing
In any weather
By a silver barn
Is an emerald feather.

My heart grows breathless
When I pass by
A young tree reaching
Toward a golden sky,

Or stretching upward,
Brave and proud,
To toss its branches
Against a cloud.

'Something of God'

WALT WHITMAN

I see something of God each hour of the twenty-four, and each moment then,

In the faces of men and women I see God, and in my own face in the glass,

I find letters from God dropped in the street—and every one is signed by God's name,

And I leave them where they are, for I know that others will punctually come forever and ever.

There are two ways of spreading light:
to be the candle
or the mirror that reflects it.

EDITH WHARTON

Look for a lovely thing and you will find it.

SARA TEASDALE

Let there be many windows in your soul,
That all the glory of the universe
May beautify it.

ELLA WHEELER WILCOX

We Thank Thee

RALPH WALDO EMERSON

For flowers that bloom about our feet;
For tender grass so fresh and sweet;
For song of bird and hum of bee;
For all things fair we hear and see,
Father in Heaven, we thank Thee!

The Right Kind of People

EDWIN MARKHAM

Gone is the city, gone the day,
Yet still the story and the meaning stay:

Once where a prophet in the palm shade basked
A traveler chanced at noon to rest his mules.
"What sort of people may they be," he asked,
"In this proud city on the plains o'erspread?"
"Well, friend, what sort of people whence you came?"
"What sort?" the packman scowled;
"Why, knaves and fools."
"You'll find the people here the same,"
The wise man said.

Another stranger in the dusk drew near,
And pausing, cried "What sort of people here
In your bright city where yon towers arise?"
"Well, friend, what sort of people whence you came?"
"What sort?" the pilgrim smiled,
"Good, true and wise."
"You'll find the people here the same,"
The wise man said.

Good Morning, America / CARL SANDBURG

*S*ea sunsets give us keepsakes.
Prairie gloamings, pay us for prayers.
Mountain clouds on bronze skies—Give us great memories.
Let us have summer roses.
Let us have tawny harvest haze in pumpkin time.
Let us have springtime faces to toil for and play for.
Let us have the fun of booming winds on long waters.
Give us dreamy blue twilights—of winter evenings—
   to wrap us in a coat of dreaminess.
Moonlight, come down—shine down, moonlight—
   meet every bird cry and every song calling
   to a hard old earth, a sweet young earth.

The Swing

ROBERT LOUIS STEVENSON

How do you like to go up in a swing,
Up in the air so blue?
Oh, I do think it the pleasantest thing
Ever a child can do!

Up in the air and over the wall,
Till I can see so wide,
Rivers and trees and cattle and all
Over the countryside—

Till I look down on the garden green,
Down on the roof so brown—
Up in the air I go flying again,
Up in the air and down!

*Those who dream by day
are cognizant of many things which escape those
who dream only by night.*

EDGAR ALLAN POE

The Making of Friends

EDGAR A. GUEST

Life is sweet just because of the friends we have made
And the things which in common we share;
We want to live on, not just for ourselves,
But because of the people who care;
It's giving and doing for somebody else...
On that all life's splendor depends,
And the joy of this world when you've summed it all up,
Is found in the making of friends.

My Heart Leaps Up

WILLIAM WORDSWORTH

My heart leaps up when I behold
A rainbow in the sky:
So was it when my life began,
So is it now I am a man,
So be it when I shall grow old
Or let me die!
The Child is father of the Man:
And I could wish my days to be
Bound each to each by natural piety.

The Greatest Thing in the World

HENRY DRUMMOND

"Love," urges Paul, "never faileth." Then he begins one of his marvellous lists of the great things of the day, and exposes them one by one. He runs over the things that men thought were going to last, and shows that they are all fleeting.

He did not mention money, fortune, fame; but he picked out the great things of his time, the things the best men thought had something in them, and brushed them peremptorily aside. Paul had no charge against these things in themselves. All he said about them was that they would not last. They were great things, but not supreme things. There were things beyond them. What we are stretches past what we do, beyond what we possess....There is a great deal in the world that is delightful and beautiful...but it will not last. Nothing that it contains is worth the life and consecration of an immortal soul. The immortal soul must give itself to something that is immortal. And the only immortal things are these: "Now abideth faith, hope, love, but the greatest of these is love."

Some think the time will come when two of these three things will also pass away—faith into sight, and hope into fruition. Paul does not say so. We know but little now about the conditions of the life that is to come. But what is certain is that Love must last. God, the Eternal God, is Love. Covet therefore that everlasting gift, that one thing which it is certain is going to stand, that one coinage which will be current in the Universe when all the other coinages of all the nations of the world shall be useless and unhonored. You will give

yourselves to many things, give yourselves first to Love. *Hold things in their proportion.* Let at least the first great object of our lives be to achieve the character defended in these words, the character—and it is the character of Christ—which is built around Love.

I have said this thing is eternal. . . . I was not told when I was a boy that "God so loved the world that He gave His only begotten Son, that whosoever believeth in Him should have everlasting life." What I was told, I remember, was that God so loved the world that, if I trusted in Him, I was to have a thing called peace, or I was to have rest, or I was to have joy, or I was to have safety. But I had to find out for myself that whosoever trusteth in Him—that is, whosoever loveth Him, for trust is only the avenue to Love—hath everlasting *life.* The Gospel offers a man life. Never offer men a thimbleful of Gospel. Do not offer them merely joy, or merely peace, or merely rest, or merely safety; tell them how Christ came to give men a more abundant life than they have, a life abundant in love, . . . and large in enterprise for the alleviation and redemption of the world. Then only can the Gospel take hold of the whole of a man, body, soul, and spirit, and give to each part its exercise and reward. . . .

To love abundantly is to live abundantly, and to love forever is to live forever. Hence, eternal life is inextricably bound up with love. We want to live forever for the same reason that we want to live tomorrow. Why do you want to live tomorrow? It is because there is someone who loves you, and whom you want to see tomorrow, and be with, and love back. . . . It is when a man has no one to love him that he commits suicide. So long as he has friends, those who love him and whom he loves, he will live; because to live is to love. Be it but the love of a dog, it will keep him in life; but let that go and he has no contact with life, no reason to live. The "energy of life" has failed. Eternal life also is to know God, and God is love. This is Christ's own definition. Ponder it. "This is life eternal, that they might know Thee the only true God, and Jesus Christ whom Thou hast sent." Love must be eternal. It is what God is. On the last analysis, then, love is Life. Love never faileth, and life never faileth, so long as there is love. That is the philosophy of what Paul is showing us; the reason why in the nature of things Love should be the supreme thing — because it is going to last; because in the nature of things it is an Eternal Life. That Life is a thing that we are living now, not that we get when we die; that we shall have a poor chance of getting when we die unless we are living now.

"Love suffereth long, and is kind; love envieth not; love vaunteth not itself." Get these ingredients into your life. Then everything that you do is eternal. It is worth doing. It is worth giving time to. No man can become a saint in his sleep; and to fulfill the conditions required demands a certain amount of prayer and meditation and time, just as improvement in any direction, bodily or mental, requires preparation and care. Address yourself to that one thing; at any cost have this transcendent character exchanged for yours. You will find as you look back upon your life that the moments that stand out, the moments when you have really lived, are the moments when you have done things in a spirit of love. As memory scans the past, above and beyond all the transitory pleasures of life, there leap forward those supreme hours when you have been enabled to do unnoticed kindnesses to those around about you, things too trifling to speak about, but which you feel have entered into your eternal life. Every other good is visionary. But the acts of love which no man knows about, or can ever know about—they never fail.

In the Book of Matthew, where the Judgment Day is depicted for us in the imagery of One seated upon a throne, and dividing the sheep from the goats, the test of a man then is not, "How have I believed?" but "How have I loved?" The test of religion, the final test of religion, is not religiousness, but Love. I say the final test of religion at that great Day is not religiousness, but Love; not what I have done, not what I have believed, not what I have achieved, but how I have discharged the common charities of life. Sins of commission in that awful indictment are not even referred to. By what we

have not done, *by sins of omission,* we are judged. It could not be otherwise. For the withholding of love is the negation of the spirit of Christ, the proof that we never knew Him, that for us He lived in vain. It means that He suggested nothing in all our thoughts, that He inspired nothing in all our lives, that we were not once near enough to Him to be seized with the spell of His compassion for the world. It means that:

> *"I lived for myself, I thought for myself,*
> *For myself, and none beside —*
> *Just as if Jesus had never lived,*
> *As if He had never died."*

It is the Son of *Man* before whom the nations of the world shall be gathered. It is in the presence of *Humanity* that we shall be charged. ...Those will be there whom we have met and helped; or there, the unpitied multitude whom we neglected or despised. No other Witness need be summoned. No other charge than lovelessness shall be preferred. Be not deceived. The words which all of us shall one Day hear, sound not of theology but of life ... of the hungry and the poor, not of creeds and doctrines but of shelter and clothing, of cups of cold water in the name of Christ ... Who is Christ? He who fed the hungry, clothed the naked, visited the sick. And where is Christ? Where? — whoso shall receive a little child in My name receiveth Me. And who are Christ's? Everyone that loveth is born of God.

The House by the Side of the Road

SAM WALTER FOSS

There are hermit souls that live withdrawn
In the peace of their self-content;
There are souls, like stars, that dwell apart,
In a fellowless firmament;
There are pioneer souls that blaze their paths
Where highways never ran;
But let me live by the side of the road
And be a friend to man.

Let me live in a house by the side of the road,
Where the race of men go by —
The men who are good and the men who are bad,
As good and as bad as I.
I would not sit in the scorner's seat,
Or hurl the cynic's ban;
Let me live in a house by the side of the road
And be a friend to man.

Worship Without Words

HENRY WADSWORTH LONGFELLOW

Enter! the pavement carpeted with leaves,
Gives back a softened echo to thy tread!
Listen! the choir is singing; all the birds,
In leafy galleries beneath the eaves,
Are singing! listen, ere the sound be fled,
And learn there may be worship without words.

No man is an island, entire of itself;
every man is a piece of the continent,
a part of the maine.

JOHN DONNE

A thing of beauty is a joy forever.

JOHN KEATS

Look to this day!
For it is life, the very life of life.

from the SANSKRIT

Alone With Nature

ANNE FRANK

The best remedy for those who are afraid, lonely, or unhappy is to go outside, somewhere where they can be quite alone with the heavens, nature, and God. Because only then does one feel that all is as it should be and that God wishes to see people happy, amidst the simple beauty of nature. As long as this exists, and it certainly always will, I know that then there will always be comfort for every sorrow, whatever the circumstances may be.

My Heart's in the Highlands

ROBERT BURNS

My heart's in the Highlands, my heart is not here;
My heart's in the Highlands a-chasing the deer;
A-chasing the wild deer, and following the roe—
My heart's in the Highlands wherever I go.

The Lake Isle of Innisfree

WILLIAM BUTLER YEATS

I will arise and go now, and go to Innisfree,
And a small cabin build there, of clay and wattles made;
Nine bean rows will I have there, a hive for the honey bee,
And live alone in the bee-loud glade.

And I shall have some peace there, for peace comes dropping slow,
Dropping from the veils of the morning to where the cricket sings;
There midnight's all a glimmer, and noon a purple glow,
And evening full of the linnet's wings.

I will arise and go now, for always, night and day,
I hear lake-water lapping with low sounds by the shore;
While I stand on the roadway, or on the pavements gray,
I hear it in the deep heart's core.

If / RUDYARD KIPLING

If you can keep your head when all about you
Are losing theirs, and blaming it on you,
If you can trust yourself when all men doubt you,
But make allowance for their doubting, too;
If you can wait and not be tired by waiting,
Or being lied about, don't deal in lies,
Or being hated, don't give way to hating,
And yet don't look too good nor talk too wise;

If you can dream and not make dreams your master,
If you can think, and not make thoughts your aim,
If you can meet with triumph and disaster,
And treat those two impostors just the same;
If you can bear to hear the truth you've spoken
Twisted by knaves to make a trap for fools,
Or watch the things you gave your life to, broken,
And stoop and build 'em up with worn-out tools;

If you can make one heap of all your winnings,
And risk it on one turn of pitch-and-toss,
And lose, and start again at your beginnings,
And never breathe a word about your loss;
If you can force your heart and nerve and sinew
To serve your turn long after they are gone,
And so hold on when there is nothing in you
Except the will which says to them: "Hold on!"

If you can talk with crowds and keep your virtue,
Or walk with kings—nor lose the common touch,
If neither foes nor loving friends can hurt you,
If all men count with you, but none too much;
If you can fill the unforgiving minute
With sixty seconds' worth of distance run,
Yours is the Earth and everything that's in it,
And—which is more—you'll be a Man, my Son!

Happiness is a butterfly, which when pursued

s always just beyond your grasp, but which,

if you will sit down quietly, may alight upon you.

NATHANIEL HAWTHORNE

Sea Fever

JOHN MASEFIELD

I must go down to the seas again, to the lonely sea and the sky,
And all I ask is a tall ship and a star to steer her by;
And the wheel's kick and the wind's song and the white sail's shaking,
And a grey mist on the sea's face, and a grey dawn breaking.

I must go down to the seas again, for the call of the running tide
Is a wild call and a clear call that may not be denied;
And all I ask is a windy day with the white clouds flying,
And the flung spray and the blown spume, and the sea-gulls crying.

I must go down to the seas again, to the vagrant gypsy life,
To the gull's way and the whale's way where the wind's like a whetted knife;
And all I ask is a merry yarn from a laughing fellow-rover,
And quiet sleep and a sweet dream when the long trick's over.

A Psalm of Trust

PSALM 121

I will lift up mine eyes unto the hills, from whence cometh my help.

My help *cometh* from the LORD, which made heaven and earth.

He will not suffer thy foot to be moved: he that keepeth thee will not slumber.

Behold, he that keepeth Israel shall neither slumber nor sleep.

The LORD *is* thy keeper: the LORD *is* thy shade upon thy right hand.

The sun shall not smite thee by day, nor the moon by night.

The LORD shall preserve thee from all evil: he shall preserve thy soul.

The LORD shall preserve thy going out and thy coming in from this time forth, and even for evermore.

Keep your face to the sunshine

and you cannot see the shadow.

HELEN KELLER

Clear Skies Again

BORIS PASTERNAK

The lake is one enormous bowl.
The sky—a multitude of clouds
Like piles of mountain glaciers risen
Immovably in dazzling crowds.

In veering daytime light the woods
Seem new and changeful, not the same:
One moment deep in murky shadows,
On a sudden like a torch aflame.

When, after days of stormy weather,
Between the clouds looks out the vast
Blue sky, how festive in their triumph
The lowly grass and fields at last!

The winds lie still in calmer air;
The sun is kindred to the grass;
The leaves in light transparent glisten
Like figures etched in colored glass.

In the stained windows of the church
True prophet, saint, and holy wife
In shining crowns, unsleeping, keep
Their vigil with eternal life.

I feel the dim cathedral nave
Grow vaster, infinite with calm,
And hear far choirs in the spheres
Ring out in one triumphant psalm.

O World, O Life, immortal Time!
I will now in secret adoration
Live, trembling, faithful in your service
With tears of joy and exaltation.

Vision

KAHLIL GIBRAN

*W*hen Night came and Slumber spread its garment upon the face of the earth, I left my bed and walked toward the sea saying, *"The sea never sleeps, and in its vigil there is consolation for a sleepless soul."* The mist from the mountains had engauzed the region as a veil adorns the face of a young woman. I gazed at the teeming waves and listened to their praise of God and meditated upon the eternal power hidden within them — that power which runs with the tempest and rises with the volcano and smiles through the lips of the roses and sings with the brooks. Then I saw three phantoms sitting upon a rock. I stumbled toward them as if some power were pulling me against my will. Within a few paces from the phantoms, I halted as though held still by a magic force.

At that moment one of the phantoms stood up and in a voice that seemed to rise from the depth of the sea said: *"Life without Love is like a tree without blossom and fruit. And love without Beauty is like flowers without scent and fruit without seeds...Life, Love, and Beauty are three persons in one, who cannot be separated or changed."*

A second phantom spoke with a voice that roared like cascading water and said: *"Life without Rebellion is like seasons without Spring. And Rebellion without Right is like Spring in an arid desert...Life, Rebellion, and Right are three-in-one who cannot be changed or separated."*

Then the third phantom in a voice like a clap of thunder spoke: *"Life without Freedom is like a body without a soul, and Freedom without Thought is like a confused spirit...Life, Freedom, and Thought are three-in-one, and are everlasting and never pass away."*

Then the three phantoms stood up together and with one tremendous voice said: *"That which Love begets, that which Rebellion creates, that which Freedom rears, are three manifestations of God. And God is the expression of the intelligent Universe."* At that moment Silence mingled with the rustling of invisible wings and trembling of ethereal bodies; and it prevailed.

I closed my eyes and listened to the echoes of the sayings, which I had just heard, and when I opened them I saw nothing but the sea wreathed in mist. I walked toward the rock where the three phantoms were sitting, but I saw naught save a column of incense spiralling toward heaven.

Photographers

M. M. Baughman: *Page* 8. T. Burgeman, ALPHA, Inc.: *Page* 19(T). Simon Cherpitel: *Page* 43(B). Colour Library International: *Page* 3. James Cozad: *Pages* 6, 23. Dr. E. R. Degginger: *Pages* 5, 15, 35(R), 38(T), 44, 45, 61. Samuel DeVergilio: *Page* 12(B). Dan Driver: *Page* 43(T). Phoebe Dunn: *Pages* 7(T), 17, 26. John Egan: *Page* 4. Richard Fanolio: *Dust Jacket, Pages* 16, 22, 25, 27, 35(L), 50, 51, 52. D. Fitzgerald, FPG, Inc.: *Page* 13. Dick Gunn: *Pages* 31, 32. Dennis Hallinan, FPG, Inc.: *Pages* 20, 21. Jack Jonathan: *Pages* 34(R), 57. Fred Kautt: *Pages* 36, 37. Richard P. King: *Page* 18. Joe Klemovich: *Pages* 39, 47. Larry Knox: *Page* 46. John Kohout, Root Resources, Inc.: *Pages* 48, 49. Don McCoy, Black Star, Inc.: *Page* 34(L). Charles Mueller: *Pages* 54, 55. Josef Muench: *Pages* 38(B), 53. John Perryman: *Front Endpaper.* H. Armstrong Roberts, Inc.: *Pages* 10, 11. Lee Stork: *Page* 7(B). Three Lions, Inc.: *Page* 42. Washington Cathedral, Washington, D. C.: *Page* 41. Dr. John Weaver: *Back Endpaper, Title Page (L), Page* 12(T). L. Willinger, FPG, Inc.: *Pages* 28, 29. H. Yeager, ALPHA, Inc.: *Page* 19(B). Jack Zehrt: *Title Page(R).*

Text set in linofilm Palatino by Western Typesetting Service.
Titles set in handset Palatino italic by Rochester Typographic Company.
Designed by Ronald E. Garman.